Fractions 6th Grade Math Essentials
Children's Fraction Books

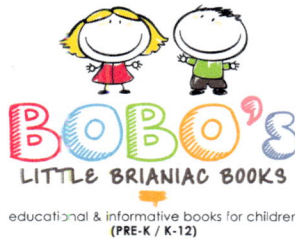

BoBo's
LITTLE BRIANIAC BOOKS

educational & informative books for children
(PRE-K / K-12)

Adding unlike fractions

1    $\dfrac{10}{11} + \dfrac{7}{12} =$ 5 $\dfrac{8}{11} + \dfrac{5}{11} =$

2    $\dfrac{8}{11} + \dfrac{11}{5} =$ 6 $\dfrac{11}{6} + \dfrac{1}{2} =$

3    $\dfrac{1}{11} + \dfrac{10}{7} =$ 7 $\dfrac{7}{11} + \dfrac{6}{10} =$

4    $\dfrac{9}{2} + \dfrac{2}{7} =$ 8 $\dfrac{7}{2} + \dfrac{3}{9} =$

9 $\dfrac{11}{9} + \dfrac{5}{7} =$ **13** $\dfrac{3}{8} + \dfrac{1}{3} =$

10 $\dfrac{1}{11} + \dfrac{7}{6} =$ **14** $\dfrac{9}{6} + \dfrac{1}{7} =$

11 $\dfrac{5}{10} + \dfrac{3}{10} =$ **15** $\dfrac{6}{5} + \dfrac{7}{10} =$

12 $\dfrac{5}{2} + \dfrac{3}{6} =$ **16** $\dfrac{11}{12} + \dfrac{3}{8} =$

17 $\dfrac{1}{3} + \dfrac{7}{2} =$

21 $\dfrac{7}{5} + \dfrac{12}{10} =$

18 $\dfrac{5}{9} + \dfrac{7}{5} =$

22 $\dfrac{6}{11} + \dfrac{10}{12} =$

19 $\dfrac{9}{8} + \dfrac{12}{10} =$

23 $\dfrac{7}{2} + \dfrac{10}{12} =$

20 $\dfrac{5}{9} + \dfrac{11}{8} =$

24 $\dfrac{5}{9} + \dfrac{1}{2} =$

Add a fraction and a mixed number

1    $\dfrac{23}{4}$ + $13\dfrac{2}{24}$ =

4    $19\dfrac{5}{7}$ + $\dfrac{18}{7}$ =

2    $\dfrac{15}{20}$ + $9\dfrac{4}{12}$ =

5    $\dfrac{7}{4}$ + $1\dfrac{7}{23}$ =

3    $10\dfrac{19}{20}$ + $\dfrac{19}{10}$ =

6    $14\dfrac{16}{20}$ + $\dfrac{12}{20}$ =

7 $\dfrac{21}{9} + 2\dfrac{3}{11} =$

12 $15\dfrac{8}{20} + \dfrac{11}{18} =$

8 $18\dfrac{16}{20} + \dfrac{10}{14} =$

13 $\dfrac{5}{7} + 15\dfrac{1}{17} =$

9 $13\dfrac{3}{14} + \dfrac{15}{7} =$

14 $\dfrac{16}{14} + 8\dfrac{17}{25} =$

10 $11\dfrac{2}{11} + \dfrac{24}{7} =$

15 $14\dfrac{3}{20} + \dfrac{2}{8} =$

11 $\dfrac{4}{12} + 10\dfrac{12}{15} =$

16 $\dfrac{6}{7} + 18\dfrac{1}{4} =$

17 $9 \dfrac{3}{7} + \dfrac{9}{2} =$

21 $\dfrac{9}{6} + 13 \dfrac{19}{23} =$

18 $\dfrac{6}{7} + 22 \dfrac{2}{4} =$

22 $7 \dfrac{1}{24} + \dfrac{19}{14} =$

19 $\dfrac{14}{11} + 9 \dfrac{7}{20} =$

23 $\dfrac{7}{3} + 20 \dfrac{9}{13} =$

20 $5 \dfrac{19}{24} + \dfrac{13}{9} =$

24 $11 \dfrac{12}{14} + \dfrac{10}{20} =$

Subtract mixed numbers

1    $7\dfrac{2}{3} \;-\; 1\dfrac{1}{8} =$

5    $19\dfrac{3}{11} \;-\; 3\dfrac{1}{8} =$

2    $14\dfrac{8}{10} \;-\; 4\dfrac{1}{2} =$

6    $15\dfrac{7}{10} \;-\; 5\dfrac{1}{12} =$

3    $20\dfrac{3}{12} \;-\; 8\dfrac{1}{2} =$

7    $23\dfrac{1}{2} \;-\; 3\dfrac{2}{4} =$

4    $16\dfrac{1}{4} \;-\; 8\dfrac{1}{2} =$

8    $6\dfrac{6}{10} \;-\; 4\dfrac{1}{7} =$

9 $13 \dfrac{1}{9} - 2 \dfrac{3}{9} =$

10 $14 \dfrac{1}{2} - 7 \dfrac{1}{2} =$

11 $6 \dfrac{3}{10} - 4 \dfrac{1}{3} =$

12 $21 \dfrac{1}{7} - 13 \dfrac{2}{7} =$

13 $14 \dfrac{1}{8} - 13 \dfrac{1}{4} =$

14 $11 \dfrac{1}{8} - 7 \dfrac{10}{11} =$

15 $14 \dfrac{2}{9} - 10 \dfrac{5}{11} =$

16 $17 \dfrac{2}{3} - 1 \dfrac{1}{9} =$

17 $10 \dfrac{1}{2} - 10 \dfrac{1}{11} =$

21 $15 \dfrac{1}{5} - 3 \dfrac{2}{11} =$

18 $12 \dfrac{3}{8} - 11 \dfrac{6}{9} =$

22 $17 \dfrac{7}{8} - 11 \dfrac{2}{3} =$

19 $18 \dfrac{3}{11} - 4 \dfrac{2}{6} =$

23 $18 \dfrac{5}{7} - 6 \dfrac{2}{3} =$

20 $19 \dfrac{3}{6} - 17 \dfrac{1}{8} =$

24 $10 \dfrac{1}{8} - 9 \dfrac{1}{2} =$

Subtract unlike fractions

1    $\dfrac{12}{8} - \dfrac{6}{4} =$

2    $\dfrac{8}{5} - \dfrac{4}{3} =$

3    $\dfrac{6}{7} - \dfrac{2}{10} =$

4    $\dfrac{1}{9} - \dfrac{1}{10} =$

5    $\dfrac{12}{11} - \dfrac{1}{2} =$

6    $\dfrac{9}{10} - \dfrac{1}{6} =$

7    $\dfrac{8}{9} - \dfrac{1}{4} =$

8    $\dfrac{3}{2} - \dfrac{3}{9} =$

9 $\dfrac{10}{11} - \dfrac{4}{7} =$

13 $\dfrac{11}{9} - \dfrac{8}{11} =$

10 $\dfrac{2}{3} - \dfrac{1}{12} =$

14 $\dfrac{5}{3} - \dfrac{4}{11} =$

11 $\dfrac{10}{4} - \dfrac{5}{8} =$

15 $\dfrac{3}{7} - \dfrac{2}{9} =$

12 $\dfrac{7}{4} - \dfrac{3}{2} =$

16 $\dfrac{2}{6} - \dfrac{1}{11} =$

17 $\dfrac{6}{11} - \dfrac{5}{11} =$

21 $\dfrac{5}{6} - \dfrac{1}{6} =$

18 $\dfrac{7}{10} - \dfrac{6}{10} =$

22 $\dfrac{6}{5} - \dfrac{1}{7} =$

19 $\dfrac{7}{8} - \dfrac{5}{8} =$

23 $\dfrac{10}{3} - \dfrac{5}{10} =$

20 $\dfrac{11}{2} - \dfrac{7}{2} =$

24 $\dfrac{7}{6} - \dfrac{5}{6} =$

Fraction times a whole number

1 $3 \times \dfrac{5}{2} =$

5 $\dfrac{9}{10} \times 10 =$

2 $\dfrac{7}{3} \times 11 =$

6 $\dfrac{6}{4} \times 10 =$

3 $3 \times \dfrac{1}{4} =$

7 $7 \times \dfrac{10}{7} =$

4 $2 \times \dfrac{8}{5} =$

8 $\dfrac{6}{11} \times 5 =$

9 $12 \times \dfrac{4}{3} =$

13 $\dfrac{1}{6} \times 10 =$

10 $\dfrac{4}{9} \times 6 =$

14 $\dfrac{4}{5} \times 6 =$

11 $10 \times \dfrac{4}{8} =$

15 $6 \times \dfrac{1}{10} =$

12 $12 \times \dfrac{5}{8} =$

16 $\dfrac{6}{8} \times 9 =$

17 $\dfrac{11}{2} \times 11 =$

21 $\dfrac{3}{12} \times 8 =$

18 $8 \times \dfrac{9}{7} =$

22 $\dfrac{9}{12} \times 4 =$

19 $2 \times \dfrac{1}{3} =$

23 $5 \times \dfrac{1}{10} =$

20 $\dfrac{4}{3} \times 3 =$

24 $5 \times \dfrac{3}{6} =$

Fraction multiplication

1. $\dfrac{8}{3} \times \dfrac{11}{9} =$

2. $\dfrac{3}{10} \times \dfrac{6}{10} =$

3. $\dfrac{5}{11} \times \dfrac{1}{2} =$

4. $\dfrac{6}{8} \times \dfrac{4}{5} =$

5. $\dfrac{9}{2} \times \dfrac{7}{6} =$

6. $\dfrac{11}{6} \times \dfrac{12}{8} =$

7. $\dfrac{3}{6} \times \dfrac{4}{2} =$

8. $\dfrac{10}{4} \times \dfrac{1}{3} =$

9 $\dfrac{2}{12} \times \dfrac{7}{11} =$

13 $\dfrac{1}{10} \times \dfrac{9}{2} =$

10 $\dfrac{8}{10} \times \dfrac{2}{4} =$

14 $\dfrac{3}{7} \times \dfrac{4}{11} =$

11 $\dfrac{4}{8} \times \dfrac{11}{5} =$

15 $\dfrac{6}{11} \times \dfrac{5}{4} =$

12 $\dfrac{1}{7} \times \dfrac{1}{7} =$

16 $\dfrac{1}{5} \times \dfrac{8}{6} =$

17 $\dfrac{2}{6} \times \dfrac{4}{10} =$

21 $\dfrac{10}{7} \times \dfrac{7}{5} =$

18 $\dfrac{1}{10} \times \dfrac{2}{11} =$

22 $\dfrac{4}{3} \times \dfrac{6}{9} =$

19 $\dfrac{1}{7} \times \dfrac{2}{6} =$

23 $\dfrac{5}{8} \times \dfrac{10}{8} =$

20 $\dfrac{5}{12} \times \dfrac{2}{9} =$

24 $\dfrac{6}{10} \times \dfrac{9}{4} =$

Whole number divided by a fraction

1. $15 \div \dfrac{5}{7} =$

2. $9 \div \dfrac{9}{5} =$

3. $14 \div \dfrac{4}{8} =$

4. $1 \div \dfrac{4}{8} =$

5. $15 \div \dfrac{5}{12} =$

6. $12 \div \dfrac{2}{1} =$

7. $12 \div \dfrac{8}{10} =$

8. $15 \div \dfrac{5}{3} =$

9 $5 \div \dfrac{1}{5} =$ **13** $15 \div \dfrac{3}{7} =$

10 $1 \div \dfrac{10}{10} =$ **14** $13 \div \dfrac{2}{6} =$

11 $9 \div \dfrac{1}{2} =$ **15** $14 \div \dfrac{6}{12} =$

12 $10 \div \dfrac{4}{4} =$ **16** $14 \div \dfrac{2}{3} =$

17 $11 \div \dfrac{11}{2} =$

21 $3 \div \dfrac{6}{12} =$

18 $9 \div \dfrac{5}{10} =$

22 $10 \div \dfrac{7}{7} =$

19 $8 \div \dfrac{2}{9} =$

23 $4 \div \dfrac{1}{11} =$

20 $11 \div \dfrac{11}{9} =$

24 $10 \div \dfrac{1}{6} =$

Fraction divided by a fraction

1    $\dfrac{3}{8} \div \dfrac{4}{5} =$

2    $\dfrac{8}{12} \div \dfrac{4}{11} =$

3    $\dfrac{3}{8} \div \dfrac{4}{10} =$

4    $\dfrac{3}{2} \div \dfrac{9}{7} =$

5    $\dfrac{10}{12} \div \dfrac{1}{7} =$

6    $\dfrac{2}{6} \div \dfrac{1}{12} =$

7    $\dfrac{6}{10} \div \dfrac{10}{11} =$

8    $\dfrac{1}{11} \div \dfrac{9}{4} =$

9 $\dfrac{9}{6} \div \dfrac{8}{7} =$ **13** $\dfrac{9}{6} \div \dfrac{11}{7} =$

10 $\dfrac{4}{6} \div \dfrac{10}{6} =$ **14** $\dfrac{10}{7} \div \dfrac{4}{10} =$

11 $\dfrac{8}{6} \div \dfrac{1}{11} =$ **15** $\dfrac{3}{10} \div \dfrac{3}{6} =$

12 $\dfrac{1}{8} \div \dfrac{8}{3} =$ **16** $\dfrac{5}{4} \div \dfrac{1}{9} =$

17 $\dfrac{1}{5} \div \dfrac{1}{2} =$

21 $\dfrac{1}{12} \div \dfrac{9}{8} =$

18 $\dfrac{10}{6} \div \dfrac{5}{10} =$

22 $\dfrac{8}{5} \div \dfrac{10}{7} =$

19 $\dfrac{7}{9} \div \dfrac{3}{5} =$

23 $\dfrac{8}{3} \div \dfrac{8}{7} =$

20 $\dfrac{7}{5} \div \dfrac{8}{12} =$

24 $\dfrac{10}{11} \div \dfrac{11}{9} =$

Simplify fractions

1 $\dfrac{18}{33}$

2 $\dfrac{5}{5}$

3 $\dfrac{8}{12}$

4 $\dfrac{6}{15}$

5 $\dfrac{14}{49}$

6 $\dfrac{10}{40}$

7 $\dfrac{4}{20}$

11 $\dfrac{10}{20}$

8 $\dfrac{9}{24}$

12 $\dfrac{15}{21}$

9 $\dfrac{7}{21}$

13 $\dfrac{8}{60}$

10 $\dfrac{12}{14}$

14 $\dfrac{4}{16}$

Equivalent fractions

1. $\dfrac{3}{2} = \dfrac{18}{}$

2. $\dfrac{3}{15} = \dfrac{}{5}$

3. $\dfrac{2}{5} = \dfrac{}{15}$

4. $\dfrac{1}{1} = \dfrac{}{5}$

5. $\dfrac{2}{20} = \dfrac{}{10}$

6. $\dfrac{12}{} = \dfrac{3}{1}$

7 $\dfrac{6}{} = \dfrac{1}{3}$

8 $\dfrac{}{8} = \dfrac{2}{1}$

9 $\dfrac{}{15} = \dfrac{1}{1}$

10 $\dfrac{16}{} = \dfrac{4}{5}$

11 $\dfrac{}{2} = \dfrac{9}{18}$

12 $\dfrac{12}{3} = \dfrac{4}{}$

13 $\dfrac{4}{} = \dfrac{16}{20}$

14 $\dfrac{}{20} = \dfrac{3}{5}$

Convert mixed numbers to fractions

1 $14 \frac{6}{19}$

2 $19 \frac{6}{11}$

3 $4 \frac{20}{22}$

4 $19 \frac{6}{20}$

5 $10 \frac{2}{18}$

6 $11 \frac{17}{25}$

7 $4 \frac{12}{24}$

8 $10 \frac{10}{13}$

9 $14 \dfrac{1}{5}$

10 $14 \dfrac{9}{24}$

11 $12 \dfrac{18}{23}$

12 $12 \dfrac{16}{19}$

13 $19 \dfrac{12}{14}$

14 $11 \dfrac{8}{9}$

15 $12 \dfrac{5}{10}$

16 $9 \dfrac{4}{9}$

17 $16\dfrac{5}{17}$

21 $17\dfrac{22}{23}$

18 $11\dfrac{1}{2}$

22 $9\dfrac{12}{18}$

19 $14\dfrac{1}{6}$

23 $7\dfrac{6}{22}$

20 $10\dfrac{8}{24}$

24 $12\dfrac{6}{15}$

Adding unlike fractions

1	$1\frac{65}{132}$	**9**	$1\frac{59}{63}$	**17**	$3\frac{5}{6}$
2	$2\frac{51}{55}$	**10**	$1\frac{17}{66}$	**18**	$1\frac{43}{45}$
3	$1\frac{40}{77}$	**11**	$\frac{4}{5}$	**19**	$2\frac{13}{40}$
4	$4\frac{11}{14}$	**12**	3	**20**	$1\frac{67}{72}$
5	$1\frac{2}{11}$	**13**	$\frac{17}{24}$	**21**	$2\frac{3}{5}$
6	$2\frac{1}{3}$	**14**	$1\frac{9}{14}$	**22**	$1\frac{25}{66}$
7	$1\frac{13}{55}$	**15**	$1\frac{9}{10}$	**23**	$4\frac{1}{3}$
8	$3\frac{5}{6}$	**16**	$1\frac{7}{24}$	**24**	$1\frac{1}{18}$

Add a fraction and a mixed number

1	$18\frac{5}{6}$	**9**	$15\frac{5}{14}$	**17**	$13\frac{13}{14}$
2	$10\frac{1}{12}$	**10**	$14\frac{47}{77}$	**18**	$23\frac{5}{14}$
3	$12\frac{17}{20}$	**11**	$11\frac{2}{15}$	**19**	$10\frac{137}{220}$
4	$22\frac{2}{7}$	**12**	$16\frac{1}{90}$	**20**	$7\frac{17}{72}$
5	$3\frac{5}{92}$	**13**	$15\frac{92}{119}$	**21**	$15\frac{15}{46}$
6	$15\frac{2}{5}$	**14**	$9\frac{144}{175}$	**22**	$8\frac{67}{168}$
7	$4\frac{20}{33}$	**15**	$14\frac{2}{5}$	**23**	$23\frac{1}{39}$
8	$19\frac{18}{35}$	**16**	$19\frac{3}{28}$	**24**	$12\frac{5}{14}$

Subtract mixed numbers

1 $6\dfrac{13}{24}$

2 $10\dfrac{3}{10}$

3 $11\dfrac{3}{4}$

4 $7\dfrac{3}{4}$

5 $16\dfrac{13}{88}$

6 $10\dfrac{37}{60}$

7 20

8 $2\dfrac{16}{35}$

9 $10\dfrac{7}{9}$

10 7

11 $1\dfrac{29}{30}$

12 $7\dfrac{6}{7}$

13 $\dfrac{7}{8}$

14 $3\dfrac{19}{88}$

15 $3\dfrac{76}{99}$

16 $16\dfrac{5}{9}$

17 $\dfrac{9}{22}$

18 $\dfrac{17}{24}$

19 $13\dfrac{31}{33}$

20 $2\dfrac{3}{8}$

21 $12\dfrac{1}{55}$

22 $6\dfrac{5}{24}$

23 $12\dfrac{1}{21}$

24 $\dfrac{5}{8}$

Subtract unlike fractions

1 0

2 $\dfrac{4}{15}$

3 $\dfrac{23}{35}$

4 $\dfrac{1}{90}$

5 $\dfrac{13}{22}$

6 $\dfrac{11}{15}$

7 $\dfrac{23}{36}$

8 $1\dfrac{1}{6}$

9 $\dfrac{26}{77}$

10 $\dfrac{7}{12}$

11 $1\dfrac{7}{8}$

12 $\dfrac{1}{4}$

13 $\dfrac{49}{99}$

14 $1\dfrac{10}{33}$

15 $\dfrac{13}{63}$

16 $\dfrac{8}{33}$

17 $\dfrac{1}{11}$

18 $\dfrac{1}{10}$

19 $\dfrac{1}{4}$

20 2

21 $\dfrac{2}{3}$

22 $1\dfrac{2}{35}$

23 $2\dfrac{5}{6}$

24 $\dfrac{1}{3}$

Fraction times a whole number

1. $7\frac{1}{2}$
2. $25\frac{2}{3}$
3. $\frac{3}{4}$
4. $3\frac{1}{5}$
5. 9
6. 15
7. 10
8. $2\frac{8}{11}$
9. 16
10. $2\frac{2}{3}$
11. 5
12. $7\frac{1}{2}$
13. $1\frac{2}{3}$
14. $4\frac{4}{5}$
15. $\frac{3}{5}$
16. $6\frac{3}{4}$
17. $60\frac{1}{2}$
18. $10\frac{2}{7}$
19. $\frac{2}{3}$
20. 4
21. 2
22. 3
23. $\frac{1}{2}$
24. $2\frac{1}{2}$

Fraction multiplication

1. $3\frac{7}{27}$
2. $\frac{9}{50}$
3. $\frac{5}{22}$
4. $\frac{3}{5}$
5. $5\frac{1}{4}$
6. $2\frac{3}{4}$
7. 1
8. $\frac{5}{6}$
9. $\frac{7}{66}$
10. $\frac{2}{5}$
11. $1\frac{1}{10}$
12. $\frac{1}{49}$
13. $\frac{9}{20}$
14. $\frac{12}{77}$
15. $\frac{15}{22}$
16. $\frac{4}{15}$
17. $\frac{2}{15}$
18. $\frac{1}{55}$
19. $\frac{1}{21}$
20. $\frac{5}{54}$
21. 2
22. $\frac{8}{9}$
23. $\frac{25}{32}$
24. $1\frac{7}{20}$

Whole number divided by a fraction

1	21	**10**	1	**19**	36
2	5	**11**	18	**20**	9
3	28	**12**	10	**21**	6
4	2	**13**	35	**22**	10
5	36	**14**	39	**23**	44
6	6	**15**	28	**24**	60
7	15	**16**	21		
8	9	**17**	2		
9	25	**18**	18		

Fraction divided by a fraction

1	$\dfrac{15}{32}$	**11**	$14\,\dfrac{2}{3}$	**20**	$2\,\dfrac{1}{10}$
2	$1\,\dfrac{5}{6}$	**12**	$\dfrac{3}{64}$	**21**	$\dfrac{2}{27}$
3	$\dfrac{15}{16}$	**13**	$\dfrac{21}{22}$	**22**	$1\,\dfrac{3}{25}$
4	$1\,\dfrac{1}{6}$	**14**	$3\,\dfrac{4}{7}$	**23**	$2\,\dfrac{1}{3}$
5	$5\,\dfrac{5}{6}$	**15**	$\dfrac{3}{5}$	**24**	$\dfrac{90}{121}$
6	4	**16**	$11\,\dfrac{1}{4}$		
7	$\dfrac{33}{50}$	**17**	$\dfrac{2}{5}$		
8	$\dfrac{4}{99}$	**18**	$3\,\dfrac{1}{3}$		
9	$1\,\dfrac{5}{16}$	**19**	$1\,\dfrac{8}{27}$		
10	$\dfrac{2}{5}$				

Simplify fractions

1. $\dfrac{6}{11}$ 2. $\dfrac{1}{1}$

3. $\dfrac{2}{3}$ 4. $\dfrac{2}{5}$

5. $\dfrac{2}{7}$ 6. $\dfrac{1}{4}$

7. $\dfrac{1}{5}$ 8. $\dfrac{3}{8}$

9. $\dfrac{1}{3}$ 10. $\dfrac{6}{7}$

11. $\dfrac{1}{2}$ 12. $\dfrac{5}{7}$

13. $\dfrac{2}{15}$ 14. $\dfrac{1}{4}$

Equivalent fractions

1. $\dfrac{3}{2} = \dfrac{18}{12}$ 2. $\dfrac{3}{15} = \dfrac{1}{5}$

3. $\dfrac{2}{5} = \dfrac{6}{15}$ 4. $\dfrac{1}{1} = \dfrac{5}{5}$

5. $\dfrac{2}{20} = \dfrac{1}{10}$ 6. $\dfrac{12}{4} = \dfrac{3}{1}$

7. $\dfrac{6}{18} = \dfrac{1}{3}$ 8. $\dfrac{16}{8} = \dfrac{2}{1}$

9. $\dfrac{15}{15} = \dfrac{1}{1}$ 10. $\dfrac{16}{20} = \dfrac{4}{5}$

11. $\dfrac{1}{2} = \dfrac{9}{18}$ 12. $\dfrac{12}{3} = \dfrac{4}{1}$

13. $\dfrac{4}{5} = \dfrac{16}{20}$ 14. $\dfrac{12}{20} = \dfrac{3}{5}$

Convert mixed numbers to fractions

1. $\dfrac{272}{19}$ 2. $\dfrac{215}{11}$ 3. $\dfrac{54}{11}$

4. $\dfrac{193}{10}$ 5. $\dfrac{91}{9}$ 6. $\dfrac{292}{25}$

7. $\dfrac{9}{2}$ 8. $\dfrac{140}{13}$ 9. $\dfrac{71}{5}$

10. $\dfrac{115}{8}$ 11. $\dfrac{294}{23}$ 12. $\dfrac{244}{19}$

13. $\dfrac{139}{7}$ 14. $\dfrac{107}{9}$ 15. $\dfrac{25}{2}$

16. $\dfrac{85}{9}$ 17. $\dfrac{277}{17}$ 18. $\dfrac{23}{2}$

19. $\dfrac{85}{6}$ 20. $\dfrac{31}{3}$ 21. $\dfrac{413}{23}$

22. $\dfrac{29}{3}$ 23. $\dfrac{80}{11}$ 24. $\dfrac{62}{5}$

Made in the USA
Coppell, TX
18 September 2022

83334923R00026